Scorpions

NATURE'S PREDATORS

Janet Halfmann

**KIDHAVEN
PRESS**™

THOMSON

™

GALE

San Diego • Detroit • New York • San Francisco • Cleveland
New Haven, Conn. • Waterville, Maine • London • Munich

THOMSON
GALE

LIBRARY OF CONGRESS CATALOGING-IN-PUBLICATION DATA

Halfmann, Janet.
    Scorpions / by Janet Halfmann.
        p. cm. — (Nature's Predators)
    Summary: Discusses the physical characteristics, habits, and behavior of scorpions,
focusing on how they hunt and kill their prey.
    ISBN 0-7377-1390-9 (hardback : alk. paper)
    1. Scorpions—Juvenile literature. [1. Scorpions.] I. Title. II. Series.
    QL458.7 .H35 2003
    595.4'6—dc21

                        2002008899

Printed in the United States of America

Contents

Chapter 1

The Sneaky Nighttime Killer

In the quiet desert night, the scorpion secretly waits in **ambush**. Sooner or later, an insect wanders near. The scorpion cannot see it. But the scorpion knows it is there. The scorpion's sensitive legs feel the insect walking on the sand. Slowly, the scorpion moves closer. Then suddenly, it strikes. The surprised insect does not stand a chance. It becomes the scorpion's supper.

Scorpions are some of the most skillful and deadly **predators** of the night. With supersensitive legs, crushing claws, and a poisonous sting, they have been capturing **prey** under the stars for millions of years.

The earliest scorpions lived in the sea. They moved onto land 325 million years ago, long before the dinosaurs walked the earth. The twelve hundred **species,** or kinds, of scorpions living today still look much like their ancient ancestors.

Scorpions belong to a large group of animals called **arthropods**, small creatures with segmented bodies, jointed legs, and a hard outer skeleton. Other familiar arthropods are insects, centipedes, and crabs. Within the arthropod group, scorpions are in the **arachnid** class, along with spiders, ticks, and mites.

Glowing in the Dark

Scorpions possess the amazing ability to glow brightly in the dark under **ultraviolet** or **black light.** To onlookers they look like fallen stars, giving off a yellowish, greenish, or bluish glow. This glow lets scientists study scorpions at night in their natural homes without disturbing them. Scientists are not sure why scorpions glow. They think it may be to attract mates and insect prey.

When an insect meets a scorpion, size is on the scorpion's side. Many scorpions are 4 to 8 inches (10 to 20 centimeters) long, bigger than most insects and spiders and even larger than some lizards and frogs. The South African rock scorpion is the longest at 8.3 inches (21 centimeters).

Homes Around the World

Scorpions are most plentiful in deserts. But scorpions also live in **habitats** as varied as rain forests, grasslands, snowcapped mountains, seashores, caves, houses, and the cracks of pineapples. They live on every continent except Antarctica, especially in the warmer areas. As many as fifteen kinds of scorpions sometimes live and hunt in the same

Seen under ultraviolet light, a brightly glowing scorpion awaits its prey.

━━━━━━━

area. In some deserts regions they are so thick that one can be found every few steps or so.

By day most scorpions hide in burrows, crevices, under bark, and in other dark places. After the sun goes down they come out to hunt. Most are sit-and-wait ambushers, patiently waiting near their daytime hideouts for prey to come close. Others, such as the bark scorpions, wander around on trees, plants, and even in houses searching for prey to eat. A few kinds of scorpions that make their homes where it is always dark, such as deep in the rain forest, hunt both day and night.

A Namib dune scorpion devours a cricket.

Scorpions are meat eaters, or **carnivores**, and they are not fussy. They eat anything alive that they can grab and kill. Their most frequent foods are insects, spiders, and other scorpions. Scorpion diets also include snails, earthworms, termites, centipedes, millipedes, snakes, lizards, and rodents.

Scorpion Bodies

The scorpion's body has two main parts. A short **cephalothorax**, or joined head and thorax, is covered by a hard plate called a **carapace**. The second part of the scorpion's body is made up of a long **abdomen**.

Most scorpions have two eyes on top of the carapace and up to five pairs along its sides. A kind of eye has even been found on the tails of several scorpions. Some species that live in caves, however, have no eyes at all. Even scorpions with many eyes cannot see well, and they do not use them to find prey. Instead, their eyes help them to tell day from night and to get around in the dark. Scientists think scorpions use shadows cast by the stars to help them find their way.

The scorpion's long abdomen is divided into two parts. The first part is wide and has structures for breathing, reproduction, and digestion. On the underside is an important pair of sense organs, called **pectines**, that only scorpions have. Each pecten looks like a comb with teeth. The teeth sweep the ground as the scorpion walks. Thousands of pegs on

A close-up of a scorpion head reveals two pairs of eyes.

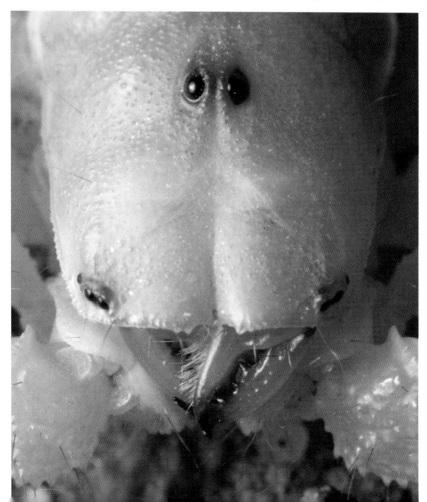

the teeth tell the scorpion about the texture of the ground. Male scorpions use the pectines to detect odors left on the ground by females, alerting them to possible mates nearby.

The Stinging Tail

The second part of the abdomen is long and slender like a tail. At its tip is the scorpion's most dreaded weapon—the **telson**, or sting. Inside the bulb-shaped sting are two sacs of poison called **venom**. Muscles pump the poison through little tubes into a sharp, curved stinger. The stinger is hollow and works much like the needle a doctor uses to give a shot. Scorpions use their sting to **paralyze** or kill enemies and prey.

The scorpion has six pairs of **appendages**, or limbs, all attached to the cephalothorax. The first pair are tiny mouth pincers, called **chelicerae**. Tiny teeth on the chelicerae rip prey into bits and pieces. The chelicerae also are used for tasting and grooming.

The second pair of appendages, called **pedipalps**, look like arms with lobster claws at the end. The emperor scorpion and other large scorpions have fat, powerful pedipalps. Small scorpions, such as the Arizona bark scorpion, have slender pedipalps. The pedipalps grab and crush prey. For large scorpions, the pedipalps are the main killing tool. Large scorpions sting only if prey is large or puts up a fight.

Scorpions extend their pedipalps as they walk. Long, thin hairs on the pedipalps detect movements

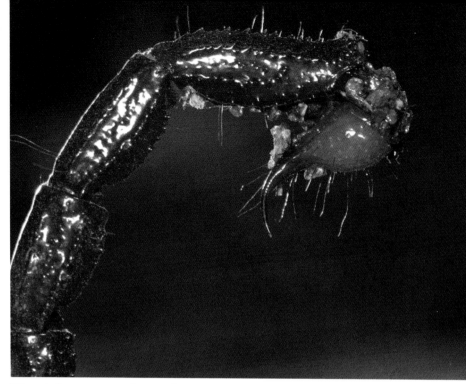

The telson, or sting, of a scorpion holds two sacs of deadly poison.

in the air made by flying insects. The hairs also guide the pedipalps to their target as they grab prey.

Feeling with Sensitive Legs

The last four pairs of appendages are walking legs, with claws at the ends. The claws help the scorpion grip the surface as it walks.

The scorpion's sensitive legs are extremely important in the hunt. Slits and hairs at the ends of the legs feel the ground move as an insect burrows or walks nearby. Using these leg signals, the scorpion can pinpoint the direction and distance of prey up to twenty inches (fifty centimeters) away.

Scorpions rarely venture out during a full moon, preferring to hunt in the dark.

Easy to Satisfy

Scorpions do not need to eat every night. In fact, more than half the nights they stay in their hideouts where it is safer. Most scorpions hunt primarily during warm months when prey is plentiful. Scorpions tend to be inactive during extreme heat or when it is cold. They prefer to hunt on moonless nights when predators cannot see them as well.

Scorpions can skip days or even months of hunting for several reasons. They can eat big meals—enough to gain one-third of their body weight at one time. Such large meals may take several hours to **digest**. Scorpions move around very little, so energy from their food lasts a long time. Some scorpions can survive without food for a year.

Scorpions also require little water. That is important because many scorpions live in desert areas where water is scarce. A waxy layer covering the **exoskeleton** traps water inside their bodies. And scorpions do not sweat. Instead, they keep cool by spending daytime hours in retreats away from the heat of the sun. Even the wastes of scorpions are a dry powder. With such low water needs, scorpions generally can get enough from juicy insects or spiders.

Scorpions are able to survive other extreme conditions. Those living in the desert can withstand greater heat than most other desert arthropods. At the other extreme, the striped bark scorpion can partly freeze and thaw out again. Some scorpions living at the seashore can live underwater for up to two days.

With their slow lifestyles and few needs, scorpions live a long time. Most spiders and insects survive only one season, but scorpions generally live two to ten years. Some kinds can even live twenty-five years. Such a long life gives the scorpion many nights to hunt under the stars.

Chapter 2

Hunting by Touch

When the sun goes down on warm, windless nights, scorpions around the world crawl from hiding places to find supper. The hours before midnight are the busiest. The majority of scorpions crawl from underground burrows or tunnels—in deserts, forests, and grasslands.

The giant sand scorpion that lives in the dunes of the Mojave Desert of southern California is a typical ambush predator. It is pale yellow like the color of sand and is about 3 inches (7.6 centimeters) long. As the sun sets and the hot desert cools, it crawls from its long burrow under the ground. Special hairy brushes called sand combs on its long, flat feet let it walk across the sand like it is wearing snowshoes. It walks a short way, then stops. Motionless, it waits in the quiet night, its eight legs spread out in a circle on the sand.

After a long wait, the scorpion's legs suddenly tense. They feel vibrations or movements from an insect crawling on the sand. But how far away is it, and in which direction? The scorpion has two different devices on its legs for answering these questions. They work like this: Moving insects cause waves that travel through the sand, and ripples that move across its surface. Numerous hairs on the scorpion's feet feel the waves, and slit sense organs just above its feet pick up the ripples. The waves indicate an insect close by, and the ripples a prey farther away. The vibrations also tell the scorpion the prey's direction.

Sensing the location of a meal through its legs, a thick-tailed scorpion is on the move.

The legs closest to the insect feel the vibrations first, so the scorpion knows to turn that way.

Quickly, the sand scorpion spins in the direction of the prey. It walks with its pedipalps extended and claws open. Alternately, it walks and stops to "listen" with its legs. Gradually, its legs pinpoint the prey's location more and more precisely. As the scorpion draws closer to the insect, its pedipalps take on added importance. Their long, thin hairs pick up the slightest sounds and air movements coming from the prey. The pedipalps zero in on the target, and in a flash, the surprised insect is in the scorpion's clutches.

A scorpion preys on a katydid.

Sometimes the ambushing scorpion does not have to work so hard. An insect may fly or crawl so close that it is within reach of the scorpion's claws. Then, when its legs and pedipalps detect the insect's movements, all the scorpion has to do is turn and grab, all in one fell swoop.

Some burrowing scorpions stay in their burrows to hunt. "Doorkeeping" scorpions sit in the entrance and grab prey as it happens by. The swollenstinger scorpion of the United States and Mexico is even more of a homebody. It does not even go to the door, but stays put within its burrow and waits for unlucky prey to crawl or fall in.

Family Team

Most scorpions hunt alone, but a few kinds, such as the female emperor scorpion of West Africa, may work together with their young. The large, shiny black emperor scorpions make their homes in burrows in the rain forest. The young stay with their mother for one to two years.

The mother stations herself in the main burrow entrance and the young wait in smaller side openings. Several youngsters gang up to grab and sting large prey, such as a moth. And if the moth puts up a fight, more young come from the burrow to sting the prey. On the other hand, a really huge and scary mantis may send all of the young scurrying back into the safety of the burrow. Then mother takes over, grabbing and crushing the mantis for supper.

Emperor scorpions often work with their young to catch prey.

The Wanderers

Other kinds of scorpions are more active hunters. They wander about in search of prey. These roaming hunters are generally smaller and quicker than ambushers. Many of them are climbers, and they tend to have more powerful poison.

The bark scorpions of the Americas are wanderers. They measure from 1 to 3 inches (2.5 to 7.6 centimeters) long and hide in cracks and crevices during the day. The most common scorpion in the United States belongs to this group. Called the striped bark scorpion, it is usually yellowish brown with two dark stripes. Its cousin, the Arizona bark scorpion, is the only scorpion in the United States with poison considered deadly to people. It ranges in color from tan to brownish yellow. It is also common and lives in the southwestern United States, especially Arizona. Many bark scorpions also live in Mexico and Central and South America. Mexico has several deadly species.

At night bark scorpions crawl from their hideouts under loose bark, rocks, logs, woodpiles, and other surface objects—and even from hiding places

A baby bark scorpion rides atop its mother.

in houses. They prowl for insects along the ground, over rocks, up plants and trees, and across floors and ceilings. Often, they snatch insects right out of the air.

Wandering scorpions also hunt in other parts of the world. In Australia the Malaysian tinybrown scorpion lives and hunts in pine trees up to 130 feet (40 meters) above the ground. In Africa, lesser thick-tailed scorpions crawl about on the branches of young **acacia** trees looking for prey. Fifty scorpions might hunt in a single tree.

As they hunt, wandering scorpions walk or run with their pedipalps outstretched. The long moving hairs on the pedipalps act like little receiving sets, picking up the slightest movements from flying or crawling insects. The tail is held high and arched forward, ready to strike. As soon as the pedipalps touch an insect, the tail whips down and the stinger jabs the prey.

Other Hunting Grounds

In Mexico and other places, some species of scorpions live and hunt in caves. One cave-dwelling scorpion was found more than a half mile (0.8 kilometer) below ground. Cave-dwelling scorpions often have tiny eyes or no eyes at all. Many are colorless and have thin, long legs and pedipalps. In the dark of the cave, they hunt day and night.

Scorpions also hunt on seashores around the world. These tiny scorpions hunt in rhythm with the **tides**. They feast on the plentiful food brought

Scorpions live in many different places, from underground caves to seashores.

from the sea by the tide waters. In the Gulf of California, large numbers of tiny, golden-yellow scorpions with dark marbling follow the water line as the tide changes. They eat mostly wood lice, but also ants, spiders, pseudoscorpions, and other scorpions. Most scorpions that live by the sea hide in retreats high on the shore, but a small Chinese scorpion chooses a different shelter. It hides under rocks that get covered every day by the high tide waters.

The sawfinger scorpions of the western United States and Mexico and the South African rock scorpions live and hunt only on rocks. These scorpions look like they have been squashed. Their bodies, legs, and pedipalps are long and flat to hunt prey in cracks and crevices. Stiff spines and long curved claws on their feet give them a strong grip on the rough rocks. They can move rapidly, even upside down. The adults live and hunt in the larger cracks, and the young in the smaller ones. Sometimes, every crack or crevice in a rock slide or on a rocky slope holds a scorpion.

In the grasslands of South America, Brazilian yellow scorpions live right in the middle of their food. They live and hunt in termite mounds, as do several other species in other parts of the world. The scorpions move around inside the termite mound and pick a promising spot to stop. Then as termites walk by, the scorpions grab them. Scorpions can spend their whole lives within a termite mound and have plenty of food.

Chapter 3

The Kill and the Feast

Once a scorpion grabs its prey, it has little chance of escape. Many scorpions, such as the giant sand scorpion and emperor scorpion, have large pedipalps with strong, toothed claws at the ends. These claws can easily crack and mash the hard shells of insects, spiders, and other prey. Only if a prey is large or puts up a fight do scorpions with large claws use their poisonous sting to subdue it. A female African burrowing scorpion was able to pick up an object twenty times her weight—using just one pedipalp. Youngsters of scorpions with large claws do sting, however, because they are too small to subdue prey using just their pedipalps.

On the other hand, bark scorpions and other scorpions with small, thin pedipalps are quick to sting. Their pedipalps are too weak to crush prey, so they tend to have strong poisons. As soon as the

Pedipalps help a scorpion to sense prey and attack.

pedipalps locate a prey, the tail thrusts down and the sharp, curved stinger pierces the victim. Muscles squeeze poison from two venom glands into the stinger, which injects it into the wound. The scorpion stings repeatedly until the prey stops struggling. By using the sting, these smaller scorpions can capture prey as large as themselves.

Scorpion venom is a complex mixture of many poisons. Scientists have identified more than one hundred different poisons in scorpion venom. Each poison works against a different prey or predator. Some poisons kill or paralyze insects, others target spiders, mice, or larger animals. A scorpion poison that targets insects might be twenty-five hundred times more powerful than an **insecticide** such as DDT, yet have no effect on other animals. The most powerful scorpion poisons affect a prey's heart and breathing muscles. The scorpion can control how much venom it injects, greater doses for large prey and lesser doses for small animals.

Deadliest Poisons

The scorpions with the most powerful venoms belong to the Buthidae family. This is the largest scorpion family, with members around the world, including the bark scorpions of the Americas. However, of the more than five hundred species in this family, only about twenty-five are considered a major danger to people. Scorpions with the strongest poisons usually

A Tityus scorpion eats a baby spider.

have weak-looking pedipalps, thin bodies, and thick tails.

The member of this family with the most powerful venom is the fivekeeled gold scorpion, also known as the death stalker. It measures about 3.5 inches (9 centimeters) and lives in rocky desert regions of North Africa and the Middle East. It is usually light yellow with greenish yellow legs. By day it hides in burrows and in small hollows under rocks and ground litter. At night, it actively searches for insects and other small animals on the ground, on stone walls, and in bushes. It is quick to sting.

The slightly larger Tunisian fat-tailed scorpion lives in North Africa and Asia and is even more dangerous. Its venom is not as strong as that of the death stalker, but it delivers a much larger dose. Its sting is as poisonous as a cobra's bite. Its poison can kill a person in four hours and a dog in seven minutes. This scorpion is often found in cities and houses, and it stings in response to the slightest movement. It usually moves slowly, but can dart with quick bursts of speed.

Fierce Looking, but Mild

Large scorpions that look fierce and menacing often have the weakest poisons. A good example is the big, bulky emperor scorpion. It is shy and usually runs from danger or defends itself by using its stout, bumpy claws. Its poison is mild, and it is one of the least likely to sting. It is the most popular scorpion pet.

A fivekeeled gold scorpion, or death stalker, carries the most deadly poison of all scorpions.

The giant hairy scorpions, the largest scorpions in the United States, also have relatively mild poison. They grow to be up to 6 inches (15.2 centimeters) long and live in rocky deserts of the western United States and Mexico. These burrowing scorpions get their name from the many brown hairs on their bodies.

Liquid Supper

Once scorpions have subdued their prey, they turn it into a soupy liquid before eating it. Some scorpions

Scorpions must first turn their prey into liquid before eating it.

carry the prey into their burrow, but most eat it above ground. Prey may be killed first or eaten alive, depending on how much it struggles. Scorpions taste their prey with small pegs on their pectines and with hundreds of small hairs on their chelicerae, feet, and pedipalps. Scorpions usually position their catch so they can eat the head first. Like other arachnids, scorpions can take in only liquid food. So they must partly digest their food outside the body, a process that takes from one to several hours.

To get ready for a meal, the scorpion's claws bring the prey to its mouthparts. The mouthparts consist of a tiny mouth, the two chelicerae, and a holding tube right below them. Sharp cutting edges on the chelicerae shred and mash the prey into tiny bits. The bits and pieces go into the tube, where digestive juices pour onto them. The juices turn the prey into a soupy liquid. Brushes in the tube and on the chelicerae strain out hard parts, such as the prey's shell. The tiny mouth sucks in the soup, which is further digested inside the body. The hard parts are discarded as a small pellet. This method of digestion allows the scorpion to eat a lot at one time with very little waste.

Chapter 4

Keeping Safe from Enemies

Scorpions are well-armed and skillful predators, but many animals, especially larger ones, see them as meaty, tasty meals. Predators of scorpions include owls and other birds, lizards, bats, mice, frogs and toads, snakes, spiders, centipedes, ants, and other scorpions.

Scorpions cut down the risk of becoming something else's meal by staying out of sight. One way they do this is by blending in with their surroundings. Most scorpions are yellowish, brown, or black to blend in with the sand, soil, rocks, or wood where they live. Even scorpions within the same species often are colored differently depending on their home. For example, the color of the death stalker varies from light yellow to orange to red, according to its surroundings.

Scorpions also hide by spending most of their time in burrows, crevices, or other dark places where enemies cannot see them. Many nights, they do not even leave their hideouts to hunt, especially if the moon is bright. But some predators find them just the same. In Australia, the sand monitor lizard seeks out scorpions inside their burrows. In Africa, baboons turn over rocks during the day looking for scorpions.

On nights when the scorpion is hungry, it has no choice but to leave its hiding place and risk being spotted. Males are in the most danger because they often have to travel far to find mates. Many predators prowl through the darkness looking for a tasty meal. Owls and bats swoop down from above. The elf owl needs lots of scorpions to feed its babies—half of their diet is scorpions. Grasshopper mice also like to feast on scorpions.

A meerkat feeds on a scorpion.

Scorpions Eating Scorpions

One of the main enemies of scorpions is other scorpions. The giant sand scorpion is well known for eating its own—at times nearly half of its prey is other scorpions. Big scorpions eat smaller species and adults of most kinds eat the youngsters. Females, who usually are larger and stronger than males, sometimes eat their mates if they do not flee fast enough. In a scorpion battle, the larger scorpion usually wins. Many scorpions live where food can be scarce, so eating other scorpions helps them survive.

Young scorpions keep from being eaten in several ways. As soon as the mother scorpion gives birth, the tiny, colorless babies scramble up onto her back, right below her sting. It can be a crowded place. Scorpions have from 1 to 105 babies. The babies ride on their mother's back for about two weeks. They live off their fat, and their mother protects them until they are ready to hunt. Once on their own, the young scorpions scatter. They steer clear of the adults, including their mother, to keep from being eaten. They even come out to hunt at a different time of the night, and sometimes during different seasons, to stay safe.

Lots of Weapons

The scorpion has several tools to fight off an attacker. The main one is its powerful, stinging tail, loaded with poison. All scorpions use their stinging tail for defense. Many scorpions assume a defensive pose when threatened. They raise the back

A mother uses her stinging tail to protect her young.

end of their body off the ground, with the tail held high and curved forward, poised for the strike. This bold stance may be enough to scare off a predator.

Scorpions with large pedipalps often use them to block their body or face during an attack. At the same time, they may poke the enemy several times with their stinger. The scorpion's poison may kill or paralyze the attacker. Sometimes the force of the blow is enough to stun the enemy and let the scorpion escape. Some giant hairy scorpions and African thick-tailed scorpions can spray their poison. If the poison gets in a predator's eye, the scorpion may get away.

Threatened, a desert hairy scorpion poises to attack.

Warning Hisses

As many as 150 species of scorpions hiss to warn their enemies to stay away. They make the sounds by rubbing two parts of their body together. Forest scorpions of Asia and emperor scorpions rub a pedipalp and leg together. African thick-tailed scorpions scrape the sting on ridges of the tail. The largeclawed scorpion of Africa and Asia makes a clicking noise by banging its tail on the ground.

But scorpion stings and hisses do not bother some predators looking for a scorpion meal. Some snakes, mongooses, and spiders are immune to the effects of scorpion venoms. The shovel-nosed snake of the desert of the American Southwest not only is immune to the scorpion's poison, but eats scorpions and little else. Other predators, such as the grasshopper mouse, meerkat, and baboon, break off the scorpion's sting or entire tail to keep from being stung.

People and Scorpions

Sometimes people stumble into the scorpion's ambush or hiding place. Scorpions are generally shy and do not seek out people as a meal. But scorpions are likely to sting if a person touches or surprises them. Scorpions like to hide in shoes, bedding, firewood, and other dark places. In Texas, twenty-six scorpions were found in the folds of a small tent. People who live where there are scorpions need to take precautions, such as shaking out their shoes and bedding, not going barefoot, and wearing gloves when handling firewood.

The sting of most scorpions is no worse than that of a honeybee. But the poison of about twenty-five kinds of scorpions, including the Arizona bark scorpion, is strong enough to kill people. The world's most dangerous scorpions live in North Africa, the Middle

The shovel-nosed snake of the American Southwest preys primarily on scorpions.

East, South America, India, and Mexico. Children and the elderly are the most at risk. Medicines called **antivenins** that combat the effects of venom have greatly reduced the number of deaths from scorpion stings in recent years.

On the other hand, scorpion venom is being used to help people. The study of scorpion venom led to a medicine for treating a disease called a stroke. Scientists are studying ways scorpion venom might be used to fight other diseases, such as cancer, and to prevent **malaria**. They also are investigating the use of scorpion insect poisons as insecticides to kill harmful insects without hurting other animals.

A biologist observes a scorpion under a black light. Scorpions are being used in medical research to help fight diseases.

The scorpion has figured in the legends of peoples from earliest times. In Greek myth, a mighty hunter named Orion boasted that he could kill every animal on Earth. According to legend, the gods asked the scorpion to stop him. The scorpion did so by stinging Orion in the foot, killing him. To

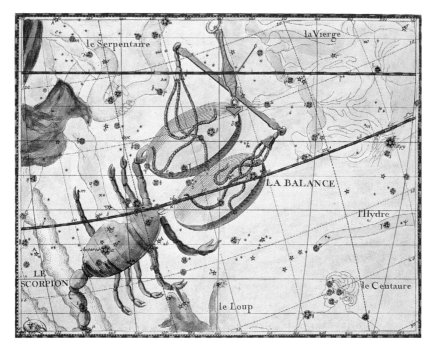

Seen in this mythological chart of the heavens, the scorpion symbolizes the constellation Scorpius.

honor the event, the gods placed the scorpion in the sky as a group of stars. The stars make up the **constellation** Scorpius.

To this day, Scorpius chases the constellation of Orion the Great Hunter across the sky. In the Northern Hemisphere, as Orion sets at the end of winter, Scorpius rises. Each summer night, Scorpius crawls across the southern sky. Down below, scorpions hunt as they have for millions of years, under the glow of their very own scorpion night-light.

Glossary

abdomen: The long second section of a scorpion.

acacia: Flowering tree that grows in warm regions.

ambush: To wait quietly for prey to appear, then attack by surprise.

antivenins: Medicines to keep an animal's poison from working.

appendages: Limbs, such as legs, joined to the main sections of the body.

arachnid: A class of arthropods having eight legs and two-part bodies.

arthropods: A group of animals without backbones that have segmented bodies, jointed legs, and a hard outer shell.

carapace: The hard plate covering the top of the front section of a scorpion.

carnivores: Animals that eat other animals.

cephalothorax: The front section of a scorpion, made up of the head and thorax (chest) joined together.

chelicerae: Small pincers near the mouth of a scorpion, used for eating and grooming.

constellation: A group of stars that forms a shape in the sky.

digest: To break down food into a form that can be used by the body.

exoskeleton: The hard protective outer shell of a scorpion.

habitats: The surroundings where animals naturally live, such as a sandy desert.

insecticide: A chemical that kills insects.

malaria: A disease spread by the bite of a certain kind of mosquito.

paralyze: To take away the power to move.

pectines: A pair of toothed sensory structures on the underside of a scorpion.

pedipalps: Armlike limbs ending in claws, used by scorpions to capture prey and for defense.

predators: Animals that hunt other animals for food.

prey: An animal hunted by another animal for food.

species: A group of closely related animals that can mate with one another.

telson: The bulb-shaped sting at the tip of the scorpion's tail.

tides: The daily rise and fall of the water level of the oceans.

ultraviolet or **black light:** Invisible light under which fluorescent objects shine brightly.

venom: The liquid poison injected by scorpions.

For Further Exploration

Philip Brownell and Gary Polis, eds., *Scorpion Biology and Research*. Oxford: Oxford University Press, 2001. Several scientists discuss current research on scorpions: their anatomy, specific habitats, and finding prey.

Amanda Harman, *Scorpions*. Danbury, CT: Grolier Educational, 2001. Part of the Nature's Children series, this book is filled with information and photos about the lives and behavior of scorpions.

Paul Hillyard, *A Look Inside Spiders and Scorpions*. Pleasantville, NY: Reader's Digest Young Families, 1995. See-through windows in this captivating book reveal the inner workings of an imperial scorpion. Interesting text, photos, and illustrations provide additional information and fun facts about spiders and scorpions.

Hugh L. Keegan, *Scorpions of Medical Importance*. Jackson: University of Mississippi Press, 1980. Presents an overview of scorpion biology and life history, plus descriptions of the scorpions most dangerous to people.

Allison Lassieur, *Scorpions: The Sneaky Stingers.* Danbury, CT: Franklin Watts, 2000. Briefly describes scorpions and explains where they fit in the animal kingdom. Provides detailed looks at several scorpion species from around the world. Also introduces the reader to a scorpion scientist.

Mary Corliss Pearl, "Spiders, Ticks and Mites etc.—the Chelicerates: Scorpions," *Illustrated Encyclopedia of Wildlife.* Vol. 2. Lakeville, CT: Grey Castle, 1991. Gives an overview of scorpions around the world.

Gary A. Polis, ed., *The Biology of Scorpions.* Palo Alto, CA: Stanford University Press, 1990. Scorpion experts present a wealth of information about scorpions, from life histories to poison to predators and prey.

Laurence Pringle, *Scorpion Man: Exploring the World of Scorpions.* New York: Charles Scribner's Sons, 1994. Profiles the fascinating life and research of the late worldwide scorpion expert Gary A. Polis, who died in a boating accident in the year 2000 while on a research expedition.

Manny Rubio, *Scorpions: A Complete Pet Owner's Manual.* Hauppauge, NY: Barron's, 2000. Presents an overview of scorpion biology and life history, plus descriptions of several families.

Conrad J. Storad, *Scorpions*. Minneapolis, MN: Lerner, 1995. In easy-to-read text and photos, this book describes the world of scorpions and how they hunt and raise their young.

Periodicals

Mark Cheater, "One Good Sting," *National Wildlife*, December 2000/January 2001.

Gary A. Polis, "The Unkindest Sting of All," *Natural History*, July 1989.

Gary A. Polis, "Why I Love Scorpions," *Boys Life*, August 1992.

John F. Ross, "In the Company of Cannibals that Sting . . . and Glow," *Smithsonian*, April 1996.

Stanley C. Williams, "Scorpions of Baja California, Mexico, and Adjacent Islands," *Occasional Papers of the California Academy of Sciences*, July 2, 1980.

Internet Sources

Sara Abdulla, "Scorpion Venom to Probe Brain Cancer," *Nature.Com*, 1999. www.nature.com.

American Arachnological Society Committee on Common Names of Arachnids, "Common Names of Arachnids 2002," January 2002. http://atshq.org.

Philip H. Brownell and J. Leo van Hemmen, "How the Sand Scorpion Locates Its Prey," *American Physical Society*, March 24, 2000. www.aps.org.

Gordon Ramel, "Gordon's Scorpion Page," *The Earth Life Web*, April 20, 2002. www.earthlife.net.

Science News Online, "Pinpointing Prey," July 15, 2000. www.sciencenews.org.

Charles Seife, "The Soft Footfall That Signals Dinner," *NewScientist*, April 3, 1999. http://newscientist.com.

University of Arizona College of Agriculture and Life Sciences, "Scorpions." http://ag.arizona.edu.

Websites

Biodiversity Explorer (www.museums.org.za).

The Scorpion Emporium (http://wrbu.si.edu).

The Scorpion Files (www.ub.ntnu.no/ scorpionfiles/index.htm).

Index

Picture Credits

About the Author

Author Janet Halfmann has written many nonfiction books for children and young adults, most of them about animals and nature. They include a six-book series on wildlife habitats and several books on the lives and behavior of insects and spiders. The wonders of nature have intrigued Halfmann from the time she was a child growing up on a farm in Michigan. She is a former daily newspaper reporter, children's magazine editor, and children's activity book writer and editor. When she is not writing, Halfmann works in her garden, explores nature, and spends time with her family.